Weather Eye

Margaret Gleave

Indigo Dreams Publishing

First Edition: Weather Eye
First published in Great Britain in 2011 by:
Indigo Dreams Publishing
132 Hinckley Road
Stoney Stanton
Leicestershire
LE9 4LN

www.indigodreams.co.uk

Margaret Gleave has asserted her right under the Copyright, Designs and Patents Act 1988 to be identified as the author of this work.
©2011 Margaret Gleave

ISBN 978-1-907401-52-7

British Library Cataloguing in Publication Data. A CIP record for this book can be obtained from the British Library.

This book is sold subject to the condition that it shall not, by way of trade or otherwise, be lent, re-sold, hired out, or otherwise circulated without the author's and publisher's prior consent in any form of binding or cover other than that in which it is published and without a similar condition including this condition being imposed on the subsequent purchaser.

Designed and typeset in Palatino Linotype by Indigo Dreams.

Cover design by Ronnie Goodyer at Indigo Dreams.

Printed and bound in Great Britain by Imprint Academic, Exeter.

For John and Marika
With Love

Acknowledgements

I wish to thank Alison Chisholm for her support and encouragement and to Cynthia Kitchen and Jane Aspinall for their helpful input.

Some of these poems have appeared in *Orbis, Envoi, Norwich Writers' Circle Anthology, Ver Poets 2008 (Estonian has no future tense), Writing Magazine* and *Freelance Market News*.

The Fetch won the 2009 Sefton poetry competition. *Anomaly* won the 2010 Sefton poetry competition. Some poems have won prizes in the annual competitions of the Society of Women Writers and Journalists and some have won awards in the Ohio Poetry contests. *Wake-up Call* was runner-up in *The Yorkshire Open Poetry Competition 2009*

Also by Margaret Gleave:

Kissing the Clouds (2005)

"Margaret Gleave's is a quiet voice, and the effects she goes for are subtle. She's particularly interested in the fugitive atmospheres and the untranslatable languages of the sea and the seashore, clouds and the sky."

Doctor R.V. Bailey

"Reading Margaret Gleave's poetry is like savouring a fine wine. The initial sampling is a delight, and the aftertaste offers resonance and complexity to add extra dimensions to the experience. Margaret has an individual voice rich with precision, deep appreciation of sensory imagery, and love of language."

Alison Chisholm

"Margaret Gleave writes with insight, authority and sensitivity. Her poems penetrate beneath surface realities to reveal an innerness with persons, things, places, events which are pointed by a variety of structural controls – quatrain, terza rima are favourites – and a deft use of rhyme, especially half-rhyme. Of particular note is her use of effective imagery: here from First Fall, is a superb catalogue of description of snowflakes: "early flurries / whirl like wood-ash and splinter; "salt grains of stars"; "grace notes repeating /in the hollow dark" – how exact that "hollow"! While in Stepping out of Line – the bravado of the poem's opening line: "Sometimes it's good to bend the rules" is balanced by the use of appropriate diction coupled with adventurous imagery as "Scrawking gulls are wired to cloud, wheel white, then grey, on newsprint wings. The irony of the poem is underpinned by the fact that it is skilfully crafted by the rules controlling the use of chain-rhyme. These poems are a delight to read: a feast for the intellect, emotion and imagination."

Roger Elkin

CONTENTS

First Fall 11
No-one Thanked Him 12
Plunge 13
Pastorale 14
End Of Term Assembly 15
Waiting For The 07.47 16
On The Wrong Side Of The Tracks 17
The Fetch 18
Still Life 1 19
Ghost 20
Done Days 21
Days Like These 22
Lessons 23
Weeds Now Wrap Her Body 24
Mr Echo 25
Anomaly 26
March 28
Bellini 29
Margarita 30
Landmarks 31
Over 32
Bazaar 33
On The First Day …... 34
Isabella 35
Delft Light 36
Sea Sick 37

Estonian Has No Future Tense 38
Still Life 2 39
Anatomy Lesson 40
Wake-up Call 41
And Dust Forbids The Birds To Sing 42
Before 43
Satisfaction 44
Signature For A Latter-Day Leda 45
Changing Rooms 46
Weather Eye 47
Attention To Detail 48
Stepping Out Of Line 49
Translating 50
What We Learn 51
Confinement 52
Giorgio 53
Ω 54

Weather Eye

First Fall

We reach the wood as early flurries
whirl like wood-ash and splinter
into flash-points in our headlights.

We walk to the trees as the sky
spills out salt grains of stars.
Black limbs now flounce white frills.

Coming home, we climb our steps.
We stamp the light from our boots;
brush diamonds from shoulders.

We'll remember this night:
its grace notes repeating
in the hollow dark.

No-one Thanked Him

Every morning, even on Sundays,
Dad was first up in the splinter of cold
to conjure a blaze from banked-up fires,
polished three pairs of shoes
lined up by the settle the night before -

heavy boots for work-days, tough,
dust-grimed, hard to clean;
Mum's black rubber-soled nurse shoes,
comfortable, soundless; and my school tie-ups,
buffed to a conker-shine.

Weekends, he cleaned our Sunday Best,
an easier task; thin-soled leather,
navy blue courts and my going-to-church
black brogues with tassels.

Every winter morning I woke in the dark,
listened to frost ferns whispering at my window.
I sniffed soot-filled air.
He called when the fires were driving out the cold.
I dressed to the smell of toast,
a chair scraping on tiles, kettle clattering on the hob.
Every morning.

Plunge

I dive back forty years or more
into the black-green slow depths
beyond high banks of willow,
moss on shadowed trunks.

We dry off, swing legs
in the stream; swig spring water
from dark bottles. Straw boaters are nets
to catch tiddlers; we carry them home
in a rusty tin. Throats ache with cold.

Scuffling gravel, kicking up dust,
we hurl sticks at hazel trees;
crack the nuts with stones;
taste sweet filberts.

When we round the corner for home,
our fish are floating belly-up;
a taste of what's to come.

Pastorale

I'm lying on the moor, high above our farm
in the shelter of granite. It's June
and sunny; it's my birthday.
Exams are over and the long summer stretches.

Clouds laze across the continent of sky
and I breathe in bracken and bramble.
It's quiet on top of this world,
except for an occasional curlew call
and the far-off drone of a tractor.

Then a gun-shot.
Crows char the air. A dog
retrieves a limp brown rabbit.
I hear canvas unbuckling and the soft plop
of fur and flesh. Then silence.
I shiver; the sun goes in. The crows settle,
scavenge for a bloody piece of carrion.

I gather up my things, trudge home
in the shadows; remember
one of mum's hens pecked to death
by the other hens; the stench of blood,
feathers, a dismembered body.

End Of Term Assembly

The hymn —*And did those feet …*
the prayer; a hairy-legged, jolly-hockey prefect
reads from the Bible.

Then the lists, the good list first.
I'm usually somewhere in the middle,
escaping notice.

Detentions, late marks, conduct marks
are read out in a crescendo of disapproval,
ending fortissimo with Sandra Clough
topping the list with 6 detentions
and 15 conduct marks.

I shiver, promise myself
never to be so wicked. Yet
some part of me thrills,
wishes for one minute of twisted glory;
to be a Sandra Clough.

Waiting For The 07.47

The café is without pity, its steel seats
bolted to sticky vinyl tiles,
cracked into lines like ancient maps.

Steam rises from our black coffee;
a return ticket burns in my pocket.
Sugar sighs as it sinks in the cup.

Couples whisper, a child screams,
is hushed; somewhere
a plate or cup smashes.

Outside, rain flings grey spray
in a scribble of graffiti
on murky windows.

My train leaves first;
you wave goodbye.
We go separate ways.

On The Wrong Side Of The Tracks

We derail on the outskirts of Chester,
shuffle towards a brightly lit building.
I've no idea what day it is.
Time plays tricks here.

I try to ring you. Static crackles,
white noise on the air waves.
I think I hear you before you break up.

I am OK, a little lost.
There are so many stairs and passages.
I wish I knew the right one,
the way back to you.

I'll ring again when I get a signal.

The Fetch

I'm on a train, on my way
to finding myself, my back to the future.
My past is unspooling before me.

From square backyards grey washing waves;
rotten sheds yawn splintered doors, and upturned cans
give the finger. The canal vomits rusty trolleys,
flat tyres come up for air.

Slowing near Stafford, the lights go out;
I glimpse a smudge of almost trees,
pale humps of scribbled boulders
turn into phantom sheep. Beads of amber
string along a road.

Picking up speed; the lights come on.
A figure shambles up the aisle towards me,
a polystyrene cup in his hand.
I swear it's my double
and I search for my reflection.
Darkness stares back.

Fetch: apparition, double or ghost of a living person. A portent of death which casts no reflection in a mirror.

Still Life 1

We crunch across random shells tossed up
by last night's storm, scattered in runic signs
across a canvas of dark sand.

Birds rise as one;
flicker silver then black,
flitting above the waves.

It lies between tyre-tracks;
a cruel hook of beak, holes where eyes
once moved; a straggle of feathers
soaked and sand-drowned.

Ghost

Once, he was a complete snake,
glossed with sunlight.
Grass wiped him out -

just when he had the taste
of meat in his jaws.

His snakeness now is masked
by viridian, ochre, flake white.
Inside him, oil slithers, dilutes.

He digests the various greens
of a summer meadow; biding his time.

Done Days

In the must of leaf fall, sharp scents
of October apples take me back to Werneth Juniors.

I cross the playground marked out in squares
like chocolate slabs; up the steps to *Infants* carved
above double doors. I have a message for Miss Holt
in reception. Miniature chairs and tables
make me a giant. I can smell chalk,
unwashed jumpers, sour milk
as doll-size bottles sit near radiators.

I wander back home down the lane
along days when beech hedges loomed high,
a hiding place for bogey men.

Today I can peer over, see field stubble,
a scavenge of crows. I should smile
at those done days of picture book lies …
but I don't.

Days Like These

The woman who loved the two bantams
her father gave her – Blackie and Speckles –
knew the joy of collecting their eggs, food for elves.
She confuses barn-smells of hen corn, machine oil,
old metal and dust with a heap of feathers,
severed head , a grey membrane
over half-shuttered eyes.

The woman who gathered wild strawberries
in the dale, made wine from nettles,
fished wide depths, now lives in a house
sheltered from mud and falling rock;
the green ribbon flowing over the weir
is locked in her head, begins to blur
round the edges.

The woman who followed the sun
from hemisphere to hemisphere,
who worshipped the shrivel of violet light
now lies, a wrinkle of snake-skin
in a high-sided cot.

This woman still turns
her yellow head to the sun.

Lessons

On an anonymous day
in a forgotten season, a pale sun scrapes
the skylight, edges for attention.

The black folder of letters and diaries refuses to unzip
through three decades of rust. I hack an opening
in the stiff leather; don't need to read them.

I unfold a road map of France and Spain,
illegible at the creases. *I don't want you jabbering
in French, understand?* I listened, I learnt.

I pile everything into black bin bags,
torn scraps incinerated. Ash rises in the wind,
empty words lost to air.

Weeds Now Wrap Her Body
Ophelia modelled by Elizabeth Siddal 1852 – painting by Millais

Consider the finished picture;
Ophelia, buoyed by her dress,
floats downstream wreathed in flowers
to a sodden grave – nettles for pain,
pansies for thought, and rosemary.
A willow weeps on the bank.

Consider the true picture;
five winter months in a cold studio,
absence of landscape, a young woman
dressed in antique lace holding her pose for hours,
lies in a bath of water warmed by oil lamps.

Consider the whole picture.
The lamps go out; she's chilled to the bone,
too proud to speak, gravely ill.
She craves forgetfulness
in poppies' black sleep.

Mr Echo

She was always a bit of a flirt.
I knew that when I married her.
She's cooked her goose this time – drooling
over some self-obsessed pretty boy,
gods' gift to nymph-
omaniacs.

And my word, could she talk for Greece –
yakkety-yak from morning till night,
until the queen of mean, her, Hera,
shut her up. Now she can only repeat
the ends of what she hears.
That's you seen to
…obscene too.

Anyway, back to Toy Boy.
He won't even look at her; spends
all day bent over a pool of his own desire.
She stalks him, pines away,
reduced to bones, then a shadow of herself,
finally a whining voice repeating,
repeating. *Do not follow me*
…follow me.

Some say he killed himself
for unrequited love. All lies.
I stabbed him in the heart, and from his blood
grew a white flower, *Narcissus*
…Sissy

Anomaly

Trees are bristling with bud
as I cycle along the river bank
in a steel March evening.

Only twenty minutes from home
I hit a stone, am pitched into black water.

No cine film of life unspools;
no memories play, whirring, sticking
at the hot-spots. Nothing ...

Now, hauled backwards through a tunnel,
I'm sitting on a log, under the lean of willow.

Sirens, blue lights; walkie-talkies gabble;
water sound of divers ...*nothing we can do –
gone I'm afraid.* No-one sees me.

I drift home. Ken is on the phone;
to Mum, I think. He's crying.

Days pass. I gaze at the garden. Bin bags
labelled Oxfam line our hall. Sometimes
he sees me - a faint outline, each day strengthening.

The simmering yellow of Spring
turns to carmine plashes of summer.

October blazes ochre and copper.
I pick up a pomegranate from the kitchen table;

prick out a few seeds…
The world spins; wind rushes in, sweeps me
away down the road, hurls me
into deep caverns, underground rivers.

Earth mourns.

March

Rain slanting windows; a mother waits,
peers over the half-net curtains.
Rain on the cobbles; 4 o'clock
and Davey will soon clatter home from school.

Kettle on the hob spits beads
that play tag across the hotplate. Fish tonight for tea
and Gran is by the sink having a fag, tapping ash
into the plug-hole, her lips a thin line.

The old house settles, waiting
for a boy who'll never tidy his bedroom,
never finish his Lego space station, never
buy Maltesers at Mo's corner shop.

The trees swell their buds;
earth slakes its thirst, ferns unfurl,
cover a small boy's body;
this northern rain.

Bellini

I'm at home on a late afternoon in October.
hearing rain on pavements,
and I crave a Bellini with a Vivaldi concerto.

Back in the bar
golds and crimsons
reflect endlessly in gilded mirrors.
The barista pours peach schnapps into a flute,
adds lemon juice and grenadine,
and prosecco, a rose glow.

Largo cantabile fades away; a tenor sings
Santa Lucia. *O sole mio* competes, floats up
from a passing gondola; echoes

are amplified through air
between the high palazzi.
Walls shimmer, and the boy
polishing glasses laughs.

So many things are happening
and I'm still here with the music,
the dark, and an empty glass.

Margarita

Rim the glass with salt

Shiver in night airports,
the tired slog to the old town.

Pour tequila, triple sec and lime juice into shaker

Our room, green-shuttered,
guards its cool from the day.

Shake with cracked ice

The window protests, sheds flakes
of iron rust; opens to red-tiled roofs.

Trickle into glass

The off-key brass band tunes up
to echo of street vendors.

Drink and remember

bite of lime, crunch of ice,
tequila at the back of my throat.

Tomorrow hasn't happened yet.

Landmarks

As you come out of Copster Hill Station –
there's only one exit – you'll see a pub
on your right-

Help the Poor Struggler.
People know it as *The Smutty Duck*.
You can't miss it.

There's a Fire Station over the road.
In sunlight, its paint flashes red.
Now street lights stain it brown.

Cross over then take the next left
into Frederick Street. Keep walking.
You'll pass Number Eleven, Mrs Cummings' house.

Most days she cleans her front step,
or polishes her letter box,
a black and white cat on the window sill.

But now it's dusk and yellow light seeps
round curtains. Shadows
come and go.

If you pass high railings
you've gone too far. Backtrack
before the way becomes too narrow.

Turn right on to Clarence Avenue.
Lyndale is the last house on your left.
The wrought iron gates will be shut.

Over

A dead bird lies festering in my roses;
their sweetness masking its miasma.

Flies quicken him, a blue-green gloss;
lay eggs inside this feathered womb. Soon

the corpse will seethe with maggots white as rice
gorging on rot;

white as the rice thrown at our wedding;
white as the rice I used to bake

every day for puddings in a marriage
dead like the bird in my rose bed.

Bazaar

It's strange how they never seem to learn, you say.
We pause at the White Elephant stall.

You point to a glass case of brown trout.
*They rise to the brilliance of feathers
or get hooked by a swallow of fat worm
time after time.*

I recall,
you're thinking of taking up fishing.
You know all the terms. You certainly know
how to play them, land them.
*Use nymphs for underwater bait, dry fly
for surface fishing.*

Will you, I wonder, extract
the hook with care and let them go,
or bludgeon them to display as trophies?

I walk past a stall of costume jewellery;
most is tarnished, its glitter dulled.
I browse at the book-stall.

You are already reeling in your catch
with the lure of a brilliant smile.

On The First Day ...

God drew breath, swallowed black holes,
stitched a universe.

He juggled several balls, made executive toys,
spinning gyroscopes and centrifugal forces;

chucked a few atoms into the pot
and heated them in his eternal flame,
created elements.

Bored, he planted germs of ideas.
Some sprang up as grasses;
some grew as trees; flowers bloomed.

He breathed life into sea and swamps.
Out of the soup wriggled serpents;
feathered creatures flew the air.

From stone, the bones of earth,
he made a crude likeness of himself
then fashioned a mate.

At last he sat back on his heels
and let everything fend for itself.

What will he do next week?

Isabella
(after a painting by John Everett Millais)

She plays it safe with downcast gaze,
her long fingers caressing her hound.
She trembles before her brothers' rage;

takes a piece of pomegranate,
with its blessing of fertility
and its bloody curse.

The other guests are silent, heads bent;
pretend to eat.

Air crackles
with portents;

and a pot of basil
casts its long shadow
into the sullen room.

Delft Light

The woman, her head properly covered
in starched linen, has put aside her mending

and highlighted by sun on her broad Dutch brow,
is reading and re-reading a crumpled letter.

Her maid, half turned to the wall, clasps the envelope
and with her left hand unveils a painting of a storm at sea.

A spaniel jumps for attention.
An empty shoe points to the door.

Sea Sick

What's the matter? I said to the sea,
you're looking off colour today.

He was lack-lustre, greasy as milk slopped
over the tide-line. He picked
at edges of fish net and weed, listlessly nibbled
razor shells. Sand stayed iron smooth,
no pleats or abstract sculptures.

And that was that; he sighed,
coughed up white-bellied fish bloated
and iridescent with flies, heaved
his last and slipped away
over earth's edge.

Estonian Has No Future Tense

Wolves prowl the forest,
witches too; and farmhouses darken, dense
with smoke; doors are open, cabbage is cold in the pot.

Soldiers come in the night, in wagons, in snow;
they promise a new life over the border;
freedom bought with jewels and gold.

We go willingly, believing;
journeying farther north
to the frozen lands.

A half-packed case, a child's shoe
lie on the cold path.
Doors close

on scent of wood smoke.
The rough meal of barley gruel congeals.
Wolves feast on our pigs.

Still Life 2

The Evening Star filters
between angles of black roof-slopes
as it does every evening. I step indoors

as a last scrawl of geese scribbles
its way west to the marshlands
as it does every day at this time.

And there on the half-moon table,
the red eye of the telephone insists
its steady blink – one message.

Some truths are best unheard, unknown.
The sky darkens; the Evening Star still
fractures a drift of geese.

Anatomy Lesson

In the dim light of tallow and the stink
of grave wax, they draw and name each bone,
study how muscle flows round joint and tendon;
translate them into paint, flesh out the human form.

With block and pulley, they lift and weigh;
hack through sternum, crack each rib, peel back
skin to open up the torso; remove each organ;
note heft and mass; replacing liver, spleen *et al;*
sew up the cavity. The corpse is weighed
once more; weighs less.

The difference is
the measure of the soul.

Wake-up Call

She grew up on Cloud Nine, in cuckoo land,
blew rings round pipes of dreams, ate fairy floss,
was glued to cut-out pictures, tales of grand
princesses, castles, Disney-bright green grass.

She lived in crenellated towers, dressed up
in gold-spun straw, imagined Snow White waist
and waited for her prince, full stop
on happy-ever-after. Then the taste

turned sour; she learned that Santa was a lie.
Rats drew her coach; glass slipper didn't fit.
Her prince deserted, said he'd rather die
than marry her. 'Wise up,' he said. 'Life's shit.'

And so she spurns fool's gold for good. Instead,
embraces frogs and puts a pea to bed.

And Dust Forbids The Birds To Sing ...
Edith Sitwell

Blackbirds were the last to go.
No-one knew why or where
they went. Scientists and politicians had their theories;
newspapers blamed everything from aliens
to global warning.

After the last bass notes of doves and the demise
of the crows with their hoarse chack-chack-chackle,
their greased blue-black, lacklustre,
blackbirds were the last to go.

Imagine a shining, the warmest ivory black,
wings fluttering summer air,
tilting the world; slender strong pinions
attempting the sun, and the breast feathers,
curled, floating like smoke or chaff.

See him perching on my gatepost,
amber beads of eyes
in his restless head, three-sixty vision;
a flick, a swoop, his sunflower beak
cracks snails on stone.

Hear a song in green or blue
warbling under water, a tremolo rising,
trebling over pebbles, then, warning – attac-tac-tacca

that is the essence of blackbirds,
the last to go.

Before

Now you are nothing except
an atom of grass, of earth.

Before that you were ash, heavy in a granite urn.
I'd found you lifeless, your body
somehow diminished.

Before that you struggled to breathe,
managed to get to town with walking stick aid;
enjoyed a glass of whisky.
Before that you were a working mum;
though overweight, you could still cartwheel
down our garden.

You'd been a ballet dancer –
lithe limbs and a bird-thin body,
smiling at the camera in a posed shot,
a hand-tinted portrait.

I have photos of you as a schoolgirl
with ringlets and a pout; a toddler
frowning at the man behind the lens;
as a baby in a frilled christening gown.

But before that

Satisfaction

In my room under the eaves,
I'm writing a curse seventy seven times,
like lines in school.

May his hair fall out,
his nose turn red
and his ears turn blue.

The Stones are blasting
Out of Time on my red and cream Dansette.

May his breath shrivel trees,
his blood turn black
and his face erupt in boils.

Outside the rain throws itself
at the glass; wind claws the trees.
I'm writing my curse to the always beat
- *Get Off of my Cloud.*

Tomorrow, I'll burn my words,
hurl their ashes into the blown air;
make it happen.

Signature For A Latter-Day Leda

She sees him huddled among shreds of plastic,
cardboard and broken tiles. Last night's storm
has guttered and died. A wing shelters his head;
plumage stiff with mud, a draggled parody.

She carries him home, bathes him
in honey and oatmeal. His feathers rain gold,
plump out. He flexes cream pinions,
stretches, makes himself at home.

Primped and preened, he swans around;
and with wings spanned like an Indian headdress,
takes her to bed.

Each day he changes.
She glimpses muscled thighs, ripple
of pecs. *Cradle me, my own love.*
Croon me a white lullaby; fly us south
to a magic land.

He leaves her
a dead-end trail of footprints,
a curl of feather and a gift....

shell cracks,
heart flutters - a perfect web of feet.

Changing Rooms

It's a Saturday morning
in early December. Baubles slouch
on branches.

Angels and tinsel crowd
store fronts; gaudy red posters shout
End of Season Sale.

You see them in mirrored booths,
mothers and daughters, shrugging off
home and work.

Creased garments like sloughed skin
lie at their feet as they strip;
fit into fragrant fabrics,

a promise of glamour; feel the scratch
of new labels; re-cutting their cloth
in the spot-lit hour before lunch.

Weather Eye

King Nyakang summons his people;
works his magic to subdue the sea.

Today when our sun is at its height
the tide will be full and you can sail and catch
many fish. But tomorrow, storms will batter
our shore; the waters will be angry. Demons
will capsize your boats, strip flesh from bone.
You must sacrifice a black goat
to appease the gods and hold the tempest at bay.

And they fall down and worship him,
for he knows all things.

King Nyakang bows his head before a cowrie shell;
puts it to his ear.

However far we journey,
our sea will always be with us. Listen to its roar.

And the people believe and marvel.

King Nyakang observes tides, phases
of the moon. He marks a sacred stone; counts days
from equinox to solstice; reads hurricanes in wind
and cloud pattern. Birds flying inland signal storms.
He foretells exact events; pretends to pacify
the God of the Sea; scatters offerings
out to sea where dead ships lie. Bones, picked clean by monsters,
hang on twine outside his door
to ward off Evil Ones.

King Nyakang, because he is wise, is mighty.

Attention To Detail

I want to tell you about today -
how the beach, sky and sea are an abstract wash
of greys and browns.
Far out, waves diminish to a thin line;
how the tide will creep in, wipe out
the sand; retreat to leave a fresh, untainted stretch.

And how, close-up, despite the grey and the brown,
where sand is pock-marked with bladder wrack
and ziggurats of worm castings,
I can pick out a flash of white wings,
see colours of shells –
rose, silver, blue-black.

You just have to look.

Stepping Out Of Line

Sometimes it's good to bend the rules, escape
geometry of streets and walls; confines
of cubes and squares – all rigid, linear shapes.

Here there are curves, migrating dunes refined
and planed where thoughts can loop round trails of gull,
follow the devious path of lizard, signs

that hold their secret in the *phi* of shell,
rewriting sand, erasing at wind's whim.
So which is south or north? You cannot tell

until you climb and see horizon's rim;
earth's curvature where ocean meets the sky.
Breathe in the salt, hear west wind's thrumming spin

of spray on pewter shore at lowest tide.
It could be any season here – cold spring
or mildest winter. Scrawking gulls are wired

to cloud, wheel white, then grey, on newsprint wings.
A smudge of tanker sails from port to sea.
Dry marram grasses sift the sand and bring

a welcome break in strait-laced rules, just be
outside the lines, among the dunes – be me.

Translating

I make no sense of seaweed blots and scrawls
edging the abstract shapes of pools that shift
with every tide. I can't translate the whirls
of looping shells, and gulls' feet hieroglyphed

in sand, erased by wave, rewritten over
and over; messages that molluscs print
on bottles stay enciphered. Specks of plover
write syllables on air in code to hint

at answers just beyond the clouds, then blur.
I hear the ocean's song and almost know
each rhythm, pulse and cadence, can't quite learn
the syntax. Only when the moon sips slow

last drops of sun from sea, I recognise
the whispers of the earth, its lullabies.

What We Learn

I have returned to the place
where dreams begin.
It is filled with faces of strangers;

always dark and the moon reflected
on cobbles in narrow alleys.
Sometimes I fly. I am always lost.

Your dreams would be different.
The sun may shine on broad straight roads,
sturdy houses with hyper-green lawns.

Someone else may dream
a moorland walk, sheep on a hill,
smell of heather and a clear pebbled stream.

But I know when I wake up
in the warm kitchen,
we are not so different.

We all come to ourselves eventually;
and what we learn in our dreams
stays with us. Always.

Confinement
the Sculpture "Crouching Boy" by Michael Angelo

He chooses a square block of Carian marble, waits
for it to speak.

> *compressed by density of rock,*
> *tense as a wire about to spring*

He sits for days,
walking round, runs his fingers
along each surface, probes, feels possibilities
of flesh.

> *cramped muscles*
> *stretch, unwind*

Light flares, ripples planes. Work begins.
He knows what's inside.

> *first neck, then head,*
> *unbend a back hunched in stone.*

He chips and chisels, reveals
the power of muscled legs and arms
straining to straighten.

> *He leaves me rough, unpolished:*
agony of weight bears down,
births me.

Giorgio

With fire in his fingers, he works
the supple glass –
a mix of sand, salt and lime;
moulds hollow bowls
of amber, aqua, cobalt blue;
remembers his ancestors
were prisoners of this place;

how they added into the liquid glass
manganese; created amber city lights.
Sometimes they'd mould ships with fine-spun rigging
in full sail bound for China, via Samarkand.

Giorgio works his alchemy.
Into the lucent mix he blends
sodium for opaqueness; gold turns
to ruby red, copper to green.

He craves motion,
fashions horses rearing on hind legs,
imagines them hoofing deserts
to faraway places …

Slowly annealed in the kiln,
his art is displayed in the shop
then cocooned in bubble wrap for tourists
to nurse as they travel home.

This glass, transitioned into neither liquid
nor solid, obeys Earth's pull, tries
to drag itself free.

Ω

It's what we decide for your birthday present;
the intriguing Big-O, a horse-shoe propped on little feet,
last word in watches –

perpetual   sapphire   crystal   bezel
stainless steel   aquaterra   water resistant
to 150 metres   seamaster   chronograph.

It will be working a hundred years from now.
Listen to its tick, a low-key hum.
Look how the second hand glides around the face;

past roman numerals,
smooth mover in seventeen jewels. Look beneath,
you can see the workings –

levers gears ratchets springs bearings wheels
seconds   minutes   hours;
gift for a lifetime, the last word.

**Indigo Dreams Publishing
132, Hinckley Road
Stoney Stanton
Leicestershire
LE9 4LN
www.indigodreams.co.uk**

Papers used by Indigo Dreams are recyclable products made from wood grown in sustainable forests following the guidance of the Forest Stewardship Council.